Creative Writing

Some songs are also poems
Some poems are also jokes
Some jokes are also songs

Also by David Shrigley

Fully Coherent Plan
Weak Messages Create Bad Situations
What the Hell Are You Doing?
How Are You Feeling?

Creative Writing

by

David Shrigley

First published in Great Britain in 2026
by Canongate Books Ltd, 14 High Street, Edinburgh EH1 1TE

canongate.co.uk

1

British Library Cataloguing-in-Publication Data
A catalogue record for this book is available
on request from the British Library

ISBN 978 1 83726 636 4
Designed by Fraser Muggeridge studio
Printed and bound by CPI Group (UK) Ltd, Croydon CR0 4YY

The manufacturer's authorised representative in the EU
for product safety is BGC Sustainability & Compliance,
7 avenue du Général Leclerc, Paris 75014
(gpsr@baldwinglobalconsulting.com)

MIX
Paper | Supporting
responsible forestry
FSC® C013604

Firstly

This isn't your problem
It's my problem
Don't worry about it
I will attend to it
You needn't do anything
Just go along with it
I will sort it out
at some point

The page

The writing on the page
all over the page
makes the page look ugly
The writing on the page
all over the page
is too much
is unnecessary
There should be more space and
less writing
It would be better
The whiteness of the page
is lost
The writing on the page
all over the page
comes as a disappointment
to me
I was
hoping for a clean white page
I felt that was what I needed
and instead I get this

Crap

I spend a great deal of time
looking at meaningless crap
But there will come a time
when I won't do this any more
Because I will lose interest
and I won't look at anything at all
I will probably stare out of the window
or stare at the wall
I can feel that time approaching
It will soon be upon me
Maybe for you that time has already come
and you would rather stare at the wall
than read this

The colours of today's rainbow

Brown
Black
Dull green
Dirty yellow
Weird purple
Grey
Dark grey

Home

I fell down the stairs
I love falling down the stairs
It is exciting
and therapeutic

My résumé

I was a fisherman
I was a farmer
I was a cowboy
I was a soldier
I was a preacher
I was a teacher
I was an artist
And now I do odd jobs
and sell weed

Schedule

A hearty breakfast
Swim the entire canal network of the West Midlands
climbing over lock gates etc.
A light supper
Bed

Halfway through the wilderness

My car broke down
in the wilderness
I was wearing only socks
on my feet
and a onesie
and it was dark
and my phone was dead
and it was sleeting sideways
and it was very cold
And I was halfway through
a book that I wasn't enjoying

Enlightenment

Anglepoise lamp
I shine it on the paper
The paper that I shall draw on
The paper looks beautiful
It is illuminated
and pure
and I decide to draw nothing
and everyone is disappointed
Except God
who understands my decision

Not entirely

I saw you rescuing the dragonfly
Thank you for doing this
Some would say you are weird
and your actions
had nothing to do with kindness
But I do not subscribe to this point of view
At least

Doctor

Describe your ailments.
I'm dizzy.
I dream of monsters.
My arms hurt.
And my feet are getting bigger.
Take these pills.
Will they help?
Yes.
If they don't help should I come back?
No.

List

The tasks are various and never-ending
I descale the kettle
I buy vegetarian sausages
I bath the dog
I bath myself
I drink a can of alcohol-free cider
I do grouting
I do tidying
I do meditating
I do my exercises
I write this
and other things like it

Sheep

They provide meat
That I will not eat
They provide wool
That I will not wear
They speak a language
That I do not understand
And they stink

New will

A lavish funeral
then
My corpse
to be burned
but not the coffin (that would be a waste)
My house
to be burned
All my money
to be burned
All my possessions
to be burned

Trowel

Kept in your shed
Covered in rust
I was at your service
Now I am at no one's service
It is painful to be
a rusty trowel

Stuck

Stuck in the lift
again
For hours
– You are not stuck in the lift
– You choose to be in the lift
– For hours
– To avoid your responsibilities

Astronomy

Small moon
(I am this)
orbiting larger planet
(You are this)
I have an effect on you
But
I cannot escape from you
You look at me closely
through a telescope
I stare at you
from afar
You have not visited me
since the 1970s

Pub sign

Sign outside the pub says
Go home quietly
Do not shout or fight
Do not piss or vomit in gardens
Do not climb on parked cars
Do not set the bins alight
Or you will not be welcomed
in the pub next time
it says
We obey the sign
Except at weekends

Things

Flashing lights
Flashing
Warbling birds
Warbling
Clanking machines
Clanking
Whistling postman
Whistling
Jumping beans
Giant computer servers
Orangutans
Wind turbines
The Holy Spirit

Places

In the queue at the post office
Looking at others in the queue
Dancing at the disco
Looking at the other fools
Whittling in the shed
Looking at what I'm whittling (being careful)
On a canal boat
Looking at junkies on the towpath
On a building site
Looking at bricks
At the clown school
Looking at the clowns, of course
At Alcoholics Anonymous
Looking at the person who is speaking
Feeling empathy for her
On a road
On a journey
Not that kind of journey
A real journey

Ready

Your porridge is ready
But I did not ask for porridge
I don't care
You must eat the porridge

Medieval times

I don't want to go in the castle
The castle is rubbish
I don't want to go in the dungeon either
It's awful
You shouldn't keep people in there
NO! I don't like your suit of armour
You look like a robot
Don't make me look at the peasants
or the witches
I don't like any of it
I hate the time machine
I wish I hadn't come

Special menu

Mud gravy
Housebricks
Birds' nests

Insects
Fluff
Pond water

Sawdust
Old shoe
Unripe banana

2 courses £500
3 courses £1,000

Things I have not done

I have not broken a bone
I have not fallen in love
I have not been to India
Or to Africa
Or to South America
Or China
Or Shrewsbury
Or Australia
I have not had a homosexual encounter
I have not ridden a horse
Or waterskied
I have never done a parachute jump
Or taken hard drugs
Or had a job
Or brushed my hair

My moods explained

In the dark moments
I am reminded of the lighter moments
And I am happy
But also
In the lighter moments
I am reminded of the darker moments
And I am miserable

Quid pro quo

All the nasty things you said to me
It's okay
I forgive you
On one condition:
You paint my house

Man on the train wearing my jumper

– Your jumper?
– Yes. The same jumper as the one I have.
– I see. What did you do?
– I took a photo.
– Did he see you taking the photo?
– No. I don't think so.
– Are you sure?
(Pause)
– No. I can't be sure.

Permission

I went to the Himalayas.
For what purpose?
To see the yeti.
Did you see the yeti?
Yes. I saw him many times.
Really?
Yes.
Did you take pictures?
No.
Why not?
I was unable to ask his permission.

The child

The child said the word cunt
We all heard it
We were all affected by it
It has happened
and we must move on.

Hair stylist

I will style your hair
Like a bush
Or a pine cone
Or a bale of hay
Or an animal's tail (squirrel, horse, peacock)
Or just a big swirl
You will leave the salon feeling proud of your hair
And you will be happy
Would you like to make an appointment?

God will fight back

You cannot fight God
Lay down your weapon
Choose a different adversary
God has weapons that you don't have
You will be defeated by God
I am sure of it

Creative project

The shape of a banana
Whatever you create
it must be the shape of a banana
and look like a banana
That is the only constraint
Otherwise you are completely free
to create whatever you want
Let your imagination run wild

Dangerous playground

Huge rickety climbing frame
Easy to fall from the top
Onto hard concrete
The chute of the slide has rusty holes that will tear your skin
The swing collapses
The roundabout is like the blade on a circular saw
Broken glass is strewn around
And used hypodermic needles
And razor blades
The kids love it
and want to spend all their time there

Piss

The devils
The monsters
Their piss is dark
and terrible
The angels
Their piss is clear
Like water
you could drink it
and it would taste alright
You wouldn't want to eat their shit though

Presentation

The lights going on and off
A buzzer sounds now and again
For no reason
The toilet flushes by itself
at random intervals
The roof is leaking
There are thick curtains that smell of dust
                                        and are moving slightly
Mice are running about on the floor
Do you like it?
– I like some of it
but not all of it.

Toast

Do not put buttered bread in the toaster
Do not put pastry items in the toaster
In the event that you put buttered bread or pastry items in the
toaster and they become lodged there
Do not try to dislodge them with a metal fork while the
toaster is still plugged in
Do not put your wallet in the toaster
Do not put your wig in the toaster
Do not put fireworks in the toaster
Do not put miniature toasters (if there are such things)
in the toaster
If you cannot obey these rules then do not use the toaster
Thank you for your understanding

Durian

Is there anything as nice as the smell of the durian fruit?
But the durian smells terrible –
of rotting flesh some say?
Ah yes. Some are of that opinion. So I understand.
But I love the smell.
But what about the smell of freshly baked cakes?
That's a lovely smell.
I hate that smell. I am cake-intolerant
and I associate it
with stomach pain and unruly bowels.

Best fingers

Fit fingers
Finger exercises
Pointing
Poking
Fat fingers
Idle fingers
No pointing
Etc.

Similes

I am dark
I am light
Like a mood
I am open
I am closed
Like a pub
I am seated
I am standing
Like Mrs Ants in her pants
I am dead
I am risen
Like a penis

My reward

I have unblocked the hole
and things can now pass through it
It was blocked
and someone had to unblock it
and that someone was me
I do not require thanks
My reward is
to see things pass
through the unblocked hole

Poet

The poet drinks a bottle of wine
and falls off his chair
He lies on the floor
and thinks about his situation
This is the poet's life
He hasn't written any poetry yet

Vegans

They are everywhere
Protesting against milk
That is their right
I am not a vegan
But I admire them
I drink milk
But I do often feel oppressed by it

The sculpture

I made a sculpture babe
What kind of sculpture babe?
It was a fine sculpture babe
Was it a good sculpture babe?
It was a great sculpture babe
What was it made of babe?
It was made of sticks and glue
and it was a sculpture of you babe
Oh yes a sculpture of you babe
And where will you put the sculpture of me babe?
I haven't decided yet babe

The bricks in the wall

They are happy enough
I would imagine
You could see why they'd be reasonably content
Unless the wall was poorly maintained
over a long period
The frost could get into the mortar
and the whole wall could fall down
or get knocked down

Eulogy for dead leaves

I was asked to write it
So I did my best
I said positive things about the leaves
But really
I could not see the point
Who was going to read it?

Choking victim

I could hear him
But I could not see him
Apparently he was alright
in the end

Improvement

Unacceptable
Poor
Fair
Good
Better
Best
Better than best
Bastard

Tasks

I have no tools
with which
to perform the tasks
that have been assigned to me
so I shall improvise

Invisible

Invisible man
His predicament has always compromised
his personal safety
Never more so
Now that he is elderly
and less mobile

Responsibility

I can no longer blame the dog
for my behaviour
It is nothing to do with the dog
I must take responsibility
for my own actions
and leave the dog out of it

£100 penalty

Incurred by you
for not displaying
a valid permit
The permit you displayed
was not valid
Of course it was not valid
It was homemade
in a hasty fashion
It seems like you wanted to get fined
Did you want to get fined?

My wish

After I die
I would like all my work to get burned
I would also like all your work to get burned
Along with my work
Would that be okay with you?
It would be my dying wish
And we are dear friends
After all.

Nothing to look forward to

The sun pisses its rays on the moon
That's why the moon hides behind the earth half the time
So the earth gets the sun's piss
The sun is a bastard
And pisses on all the planets
And the moons
And everything else
The asteroids, the satellites, etc.
Jupiter is totally covered in the sun's piss
for example
Pluto isn't a planet
But it still gets pissed on
Like the rest
Pluto is a dwarf
Covered in piss
The sun is so full of piss
But eventually the sun will run out of piss
and die
But by that time
Everything will be fucked anyway

A new way of thinking

I developed it
I haven't told many people
and I have only described it
very generally
I haven't gone into detail
I engage in it
for half an hour or so
each morning
before breakfast
Then I go back to my old way of thinking
for the rest of the day

A cock-eyed way to do business

I don't think it's a cock-eyed way to do business
It's just the way I do business
It works for me
You do business your way
I'll do business my way
Okay?

Maneless horse

What do you call a horse with no mane?
Nothing. She doesn't have a name.
I said mane, not name
Oh. I misheard. Sorry. In that case I don't know.

Transaction

Would you like to buy some old rope?
How useless is it?
It is completely useless.
How much is it?
It is five hundred pounds a metre.
In that case I'll have a thousand metres.
It's in bits. Is that okay?
That's perfectly fine.

Suburbs

Full of lawns
Family cars
Kids in school uniforms
Street lights
Red-brick houses
I escaped
Then I quit drugs
Now I want to go back

Ernest Hemingway

I am a big fan.
If we were alive
I would drive him
in my van
wherever he wanted to go.
I could help him move house
Or take his unwanted stuff to the dump.

Options

Sand and
Gravel
Stones
Grit
Wood chippings
Coarse dust
Diamonds
Could I have the diamonds?
No. We ran out. They were incredibly popular.
Okay. I'll take some gravel.
Sorry. We don't have any gravel left either.
We ran out of everything except the coarse dust.
We have plenty of the coarse dust so you
can have as much as you like.
Okay. I'll just have a light sprinkling.
Ha ha ha
What's funny?
I don't know.

Zombies

I've had enough of zombies
I find them really annoying and
They cause great inconvenience
Something should be done about them
I'd suggest blowing their brains out with a shotgun
Or cutting their heads off with a sword

I do not watch the news

But I get the impression that
everything is shit
In any case
I have decided to write a news blog
Concerning the news that I am aware of
That there are roadworks
at the end of my street
That there was a car alarm going off
Yesterday
That I have a sore foot
That my dog was in a funny mood
But now seems back to her old self
That it was raining
But now it has stopped

Show your love

Perfume
in an interesting-shaped bottle
Buy it for him
Lego castle
Buy it for him
and help him assemble it
E-scooter
Buy it for yourself
and let him ride it

Yes

Buckets of water
Scoops of ice cream
Clumps of turf
Life is wonderful

Plea

I'm not gonna
Tell you what to do
Because I have no idea
What you should do
But at least
Go out the exit
Don't go out the entrance
Or at least
Use the door
Don't climb out of the window
Or at least
Open the window
Don't smash the glass
Or at least
Be careful
And don't cut yourself open
On the glass
Please
That's all I ask

In the North

Where it is cold
Down to the South
Where it is warmer
We shall drive
On a tractor
At 15 miles an hour
Or we could go on the bullet train
If you would prefer

Pecking order

I am the best
You are the second best
Doggo is joint third best
with Kitty
Mum is fourth best
Dad is number five
Algorithm is number six
Bicycle is number seven
Downstairs is number eight
Upstairs is number nine
The state and its agents are number ten

You cannot believe your eyes

Do not look at pictures of yourself
They are not you
Do not look in the mirror
It is not you in the mirror
Do not look at your reflection in the pond
It is not you in the pond
If you want to know what you look like
Then listen to the verbal description
of you
that I recorded
a few years ago
It is still very accurate
I can assure you

Parts

Head
Forehead
Knee
Kneecap
Glottis
Epiglottis
Arse
Arsehole
Brain
Brainworm
Brainworm?
Yes.
Oh dear. I had always feared this.

Bin flower

Flower growing in the bin
You pick it
And give it to me
I know where it has come from
But I say nothing
It is the thought that counts

Lucky me

Amateur hairdresser
He cut my hair
It was okay
and I did not have to pay

What time is it?

It's time for justice?
Who will administer the justice?
The judicial administrator.
Oh. That prick!
Why do you say he's a prick?
I dunno. He just really fucking annoys me.

As one door closes

Another one opens
It's disappointing
Why can't both doors remain open?
Better than both being closed
I suppose
But still …

Sincere

I would like to apologise
for all the bad things I have done
I am sorry
I am oh so very sorry
Please forgive me

I would like to apologise for breaking your windows
I would like to apologise for being drunk at the bar
I would like to apologise for digging up your garden
I would like to apologise for crashing your car

I would like to apologise for abusing your kindness
I would like to apologise for pissing on your floor
I would like to apologise for my filthy countenance
I would like to apologise for shitting at your door

I would like to apologise for shouting at strangers
I would like to apologise for ignoring the rules
I would like to apologise for brandishing my weapon
I would like to apologise for wearing your shoes

I would like to apologise for all the bad things I have done
I am sorry
I am oh so very sorry
I am most sincerely sorry

Dangerous goods

In my handbag
Dangerous goods
In my pocket
Dangerous goods sold to children
at the school gates
by me and my colleagues

Hard rain falling
onto the carport
elderly people disturbed
by the clattering sound
the grass made crisp
by the frost in the morning
I shall walk on that grass
in my bare feet right now

Clumps and sods
of earth in my bucket
there for no reason
save the need to collect
Disappointment at
the hair in your sandwich
You deserve so much better
than what you have got

Little friend

I will chew through
the electric cable
I make holes
in the easy chair
I will grab in my teeth
the valuable item
I will drag it
back to my lair
I have
a right to be here
You can't
get rid of me
I am
a protected species
and you
must accept it

The joy of movement

Slow slow
Quick quick
slow
Fast fast
very very
fast
Slow slow
tediously slow
then incredibly fast
again
all of a sudden
and try not to fall over
or drop the tray of drinks
or you will be punished
Am I making myself clear?

Master of words

I am not a master of words
much as I would like to be a master of words
Rather: words are my master
I obey words
They tell me what to do
and where to go
and what not to do
and where not to go
I am happy with this arrangement
and am grateful for it
I need guidance
for I have a dull mind

Clean place

Dirt falling from the sky
You collect it in a bucket
You are very happy
You live in a very clean place
and you see the dirt as special
But the rest of us
who live in dirty places
we think you are mad

A play

Two actors acting
First actor:
What are you doing?
Second actor:
I'm playing a part
First actor:
What kind of part?
Second actor:
A difficult part. Requiring me to completely transform myself
First actor:
You make it look so easy
Second actor:
It's much more difficult than it appears.
Anyways. What part are you playing?
First actor:
I'm not acting. This is my lunch hour
Second actor:
I see.
(End of Scene One)

Noon

At noon
I start drinking
By three
I am drunk
Whence I stop
By nine
I am sober
and I go to bed
and I sleep
and I wake up
at noon

Crushing

I like to put things in the crusher
and watch them crush
I have been doing this for some time
and now I have crushed everything I own
Except the crusher
which I also own
I would crush the crusher
if I could

Grip of myself

Pathetic hand dryer
Dries my hands so slowly
I could dry them quicker
by blowing on them myself
It is typical of so many things
these days
It filled me with rage
but then I got a grip of myself

Books

You can judge a book by its cover
If the cover is bad then the book is bad
That has been my experience
Though I have only read two books
Both by the same author

On the train

Entering a large city
I look out of the window
and I see a man
in the middle of the road
naked apart from a pair of flip flops
and a cowboy hat
singing a song
and doing a shit
The ways of the city
are a mystery to us country folk

Openness to failure

I'm open to it
as long as it's someone else's
and I can view the failure
from a safe distance
and eat popcorn
while I watch

Control the volume

Do not pump it up
Pumping it up is not acceptable
If you want to pump something up
then pump up the paddling pool in the back garden
and fill it with water
The dog is hot
and she wants to lie in it

Feelings

Feelings feelings
Feelings feelings
Feelings dulled by drugs
Speaking speaking
Difficulty speaking
due to use of drugs
Driving driving
driving quickly
knocking down a wall
Running running
into the woods
being chased by cops
That was Wednesday
Today is Thursday
Now we are in jail
Now we are in jail
Feelings feelings
Feelings dulled by jail

Tent pegs

Tent pegs falling from the sky
Falling in our eyes
We are camping
Oh yes we are camping
and the pegs are very useful
Oh so very useful
We forgot to bring tent pegs
Usually rain falls from the sky
and gets us wet
But not today
Oh no not today
It augurs well
for the rest of our holiday

New law

Eating crackers on their own is now illegal
Eating crackers alone is illegal?
No. Eating them on their own. Without cheese,
butter, jam, lard, etc.
But I love a cracker on its own. It is my joy
Well that's too bad
Your joy is over
It's the law.

Typewriter

Old-fashioned typewriter
thrown from a high window
hits the ground
with a crash
It is not the first time this has happened
nor will it be the last
Though it does happen far less frequently
these days

Repair

The machines
I know how to operate them
But I do not know how to fix them
I like it when they break
I call the repair man
I am in love with the repair man
It is common for this to happen
People often fall in love with their doctors
and their psychiatrists
and their priests
and the repair man

Writer

The words tumbled out
and onto the page
and off the page
and onto the floor
and through the cracks
and under the floor
where they were eaten slowly
by lice

Hindrances

Your ability to reason
hindered somewhat
by imbibing unhelpful substances
Your general grasp of reality
also somewhat hindered
by watching cartoons
nothing but cartoons

Impatience

I am impatient
It is a fault of mine
I cannot wait for things to happen
and when they happen
I cannot wait for them to end
I try to remind myself
to be happy in the moment
But how long is a moment?
And when will it end?

Secret

In the cupboard
on the top shelf
at the back
where only I can see
(I am very tall)
it is quite dusty
and so I know
that I have a choice to make

Moaning

The constant sound of moaning
and the clanking of chains
in the dungeon
has been keeping me awake
Please could I move
to a room
on a higher floor
Thank you

Youth

All the things that I thought were good
when I was younger
I no longer think those things are good
I think they are bad
And all the things that I thought were bad
when I was younger
I no longer think they are bad
I think they are good
I have completely changed my opinions of things
now that I am old
But I still love you
in case you were wondering

We are commencing our descent

Kindly stow your bags
replace your tray tables
move your seats to the upright position
and reset your watch
to 5000 years BC
Thank you

Request

Please assist me
in erecting this pyramid
If you have any friends
who would also like to help
move the giant stones into place
then they would be most welcome
We are somewhat short-handed

The stupidity control

The Volume Control
Controls the volume
Control your volume
Using the volume control

The Brightness Control
Controls the brightness
Control your brightness
Using the brightness control

The Stupidity Control
There is no stupidity control
Unfortunately

A nicer voice

I find your voice annoying
I am sad to tell you this
I still enjoy your company
But not your voice
Please do not speak to me any more
Otherwise you are my welcome companion
If you wish to communicate with me
please write your words down
on a piece of paper
so that I may read them
and not hear your terrible voice
When I read your words
I will hear them in my mind
as spoken in a voice other than yours
a nicer voice
such as I have sometimes heard on the radio
or in my dreams

Can't remember

In the tale of the hare and the tortoise
the two creatures have a race
and the tortoise wins
I cannot remember how this happens
It does not seem feasible in reality
I also cannot remember what point
the tale is intended to make
It may be religious
or something like that
but I really can't remember

Incorrigible weirdo

He's an incorrigible weirdo
They said
Do not sit next to him
They said
Do not talk to him
They said
Do not give him your contact details
They said
But I sat next to him
and I spoke to him
and I gave him my contact details
and now we are married

Paint splattered up the wall

– I like it.
– It is just paint splattered up the wall.
– I still like it.
– You are a degenerate.

Woman goes to the doctor
Doctor says:
How can I help you?
Woman says:
I'd like a haircut
Doctor says:
Why?
Woman says:
For medical reasons

Two slugs
First slug:
Do you ever look back at your trail of slime?
Second slug:
No. I see no point.

Day one
Bird shits on a man's head
Man is angry
Day two
Same bird shits on same man's head
Man is angry
Day three
Same bird shits on same man's head again
Man looks up and shouts at the bird:
Why me?
Bird replies:
It has become part of my routine

Baa baa black sheep
Have you any wool?
Yes sir yes sir
I am covered in wool
as you can see

Apple:
How are you feeling?
Banana:
I feel great. How do you feel?
Apple:
Anxious.
Banana:
Why?
Apple:
I think my batteries are running out.
Banana:
But Apples don't have batteries. You have pips.
Apple:
Pips?
Banana:
Yes. Like seeds. From which apple trees grow.
Apple:
Really? I didn't know that.
Banana:
Yes. It's true.
Apple:
I feel much better now.
Banana:
Good. But you're still going to get eaten.

Plate: What time is it?
Clock: Half past six.
Plate: Thanks.
Clock: What's for dinner?
Plate: Pizza. Ha ha.
Clock: Ha ha.

Shoe: Something smells funny.
Sock: I know.
Shoe: Is it you or is it me?
Sock: It's hard to tell.
Shoe: I know.
Sock: Ha ha

Two sharks swimming around close to the shore.
1st shark: Shall we eat one of the swimmers?
2nd shark: No. We had better not.
1st shark: Why not?
2nd shark: Because it would spoil their holiday.
1st shark: What about our holiday?
2nd shark: We're not on holiday. We're working.
1st shark: Working? What's our job?
2nd shark: Being sharks.
1st shark: Are we good at it?
2nd shark: Generally, yes.

Ghosts!
There are ghosts everywhere!
They are not ghosts.
They are bubbles from the bubble machine.

First man: The chickens have escaped!
Second man: They are not chickens.

Fork: What do you do?
Knife: I cut things. What do you do?
Fork: I am used to eat soup.
Knife: I think you are mistaken.
Soup is a job for a spoon.
Fork: Ah. That explains a lot.

Free beans for all citizens. Distributed by the state.
By what means?
Dropped from planes.
Dropped from planes?
No. I am joking. The beans are given out at banks,
schools and sports venues. Ha ha.
Oh. Ha ha.

I once had a boyfriend who loved me very much.
What happened?
I dumped him.
What's funny about that?
He was a clown, a professional clown.

1st corpse: How long have you been dead?
2nd corpse: Quite a while. I am almost fully
decomposed as you can see.
1st corpse: Yes. I didn't want to mention it.

A cup of tea in exchange for a bar of gold
Ha ha
Ha ha

Better the devil you know
than the devil you don't know.
Are you sure?
Yes. I am sure.

Do you think you are funny?
– Yes. I think I am quite funny.
On what basis?
– On the basis that I often think and say funny things.
Are you sure they are funny?
– Err. Well. Yes.
I don't think what you are saying now is funny.
– I do not suggest what I am saying now is funny.
Then please say something funny.
– I need to go to the toilet.

People eating noodles
– By what means?
By the usual means.

Cheese platter
– Will you eat it all?
No. I will share it with the giant mouse.
– The giant mouse?
I am joking.
– Oh. Ha ha.
Ha ha.

What's in the bag?
Never you mind what's in the bag.
But I must know.
Some things cannot be known.
You are talking about God's plan.
I just want to know what's in the bag.
Tell me.
Let me see.
Okay.
Ah. Dirty underwear.
Let me see.
Happy now?
Not really.

Drawing of a can of beer
Very lifelike

Dreaming
vividly
all night.
You do not know it was all night.
It seemed like all night.
You do not know how the night progresses
because you are asleep.
I see.
What did you dream of?
I can't remember.

Drug frenzy
– It wasn't a frenzy. It was just an indigestion tablet.
Yes. There is always some truth in what I say.

Thin man in a red suit
looks like a pencil

Man turns into a bug
Enjoys being a bug
but he turns back into a man
Man says
I want to be a bug again
God says
(something incomprehensible)

On the kebab skewer:
Vegetables
Meat
Ping pong ball
Pencil eraser
Nameless object
Now shut your eyes
and tell me what was on the kebab skewer

Men made of plasticine
running around.
How can it be?
It is a movie.

War
Between whom?
Bugs
Different bugs?
Hard to tell

Why do you jump off cliffs?
I do it
because it makes me feel alive.
Is there anything else that makes you feel alive?
I eat soup.
Cliff jumping and eating soup?
No. I was joking about the soup.

Clock: What year is it?
Steering wheel: You don't know what year it is?
Clock: I only tell the time of day.
Steering wheel: Oh. Okay. It's 1987.
Clock: Thanks.

Look at the pictures on the wall.
– Okay. I'm looking.
Do you like any of the pictures?
– No. They are all awful.
But this is the Louvre in Paris.
Is there nothing that you like?
Surely there must be something?
– No. It's all shit.

Stop grumbling.
– I'm not grumbling. I'm reciting a poem.
Oh. I'm sorry.
I thought you were grumbling.

Did you enjoy the movie?
It isn't a movie.
It's a window.
Oh. Ha ha.
Ha ha.

The world's biggest bastard
sits next to
the world's biggest idiot
in the world's worst bar.
The barman says to the idiot
What will you have?
The idiot points at the bastard and says
I'll have what he's having.

In the spaceship orbiting the earth
1st spaceman: I can see your house.
2nd spaceman: Really? Where?
1st spaceman: Only joking.
2nd spaceman: Now I feel stupid.
1st spaceman: You are stupid.

I licked the fuzz
off the mystic orb
and now I feel amazing

Instructions for the positioning of the rugs

I have not decided exactly where the rugs should go as yet
I can tell you that I definitely want them on the floor
But I cannot give you any more information at present
I need to be given time to think things through
I do not want to make a hasty decision
that I may later come to regret

Pizza
joy
contentment

etc.

Choices

choice of cunts
choice of arseholes
choice of bastards
choice of dickheads

Desire to talk versus ability to make sense

Please can you remove the serpent
from my bed chamber
I do not know why it has been put there
and I do not wish to know
but please remove it

Dancing in my cage
That's mostly all I do
I don't much like anything else

Petting zoo:
Slugs
Spiders
Scorpions
Snakes
Worms
Maggots
Teddy bear

Mud man
What is meant by this?
Likeness of a man
Like a snowman
But made of mud

Drugs

Drugs drugs drugs drugs
Drugs drugs drugs drugs
Drugs drugs drugs drugs
Drugs drugs drugs drugs
Oh wonderful drugs
Oh wonderful drugs

Drugs drugs drugs drugs
Drugs drugs drugs drugs
Drugs drugs drugs drugs
Drugs drugs drugs drugs
Oh wonderful drugs
Oh wonderful drugs

Drugs drugs drugs drugs
Drugs drugs drugs drugs
Drugs drugs drugs drugs
Drugs drugs drugs drugs
Oh wonderful drugs
Oh wonderful drugs

On a one-stringed guitar
On a one-stringed guitar
On a one-stringed guitar
There's just one string

In a one-horse town
In a one-horse town
In a one-horse town
There's just one horse

On a one-track mind
On a one-track mind
On a one-track mind
There's just one thought

On a one-armed bandit
On a one-armed bandit
On a one-armed bandit
There's just one arm

In a one-man band
In a one-man band
In a one-man band
There's just one man

Down a one-way street
Down a one-way street
Down a one-way street
There's just one way

In a one-parent family
In a one-parent family
In a one-parent family
There's just your mum

The hole

Hey you with the spade
come dig me a hole
dig it deep
dig it deep
dig it deep

Hey you with the fist
come bang on my head
bang it well
bang it strong
till it breaks

Hey you with the mouth
come say me a prayer
say it nice
say it low
say it well

Hey you with the spade
come fill in that hole
do it quick before
anyone sees

Come forward

Bastards
Come forward
Fools
Come forward
Purveyors of bush meat
Come forward
Unclean spirits
Come forward
Lap dogs
Come forward
Unicorns
Come forward
Other large mammals
Come forward
Cannibals
Come forward
Grandad
Come forward
Pangolins
Come forward
Baggage wranglers
Come forward
Prisoners
Come forward
Old age pensioners
Come forward
Passengers with children
Come forward
All other passengers
Come forward

The foreign meat

I will eat the foreign meat
Yes I will eat the foreign meat
I will eat it with my hands
I will eat it with my feet

I will eat the flame-grilled whopper
Yes I will eat the flame-grilled whopper
I will eat it for my breakfast
I will eat it for my supper

I will eat the sticky pudding
Yes I will eat the sticky pudding
I will eat it at your funeral
I will eat it at my wedding

I will eat the elephant poo
Yes I will eat the elephant poo
I will eat it in the wild
I will eat it at the zoo

I will eat the human corpse
Yes I will eat the human corpse
I will eat it with a spoon
I will eat it with a fork

I will eat the bar of soap
Yes I will eat the bar of soap
I will put it in my mouth
I will swallow it down my throat

I will eat the foreign meat
Yes I will eat the foreign meat
I will eat it with my hands
I will eat it with my feet

The diamond-encrusted skull

I want that fucking thing
I want it so badly
Give it to me
or I'm going to come over
and take it from you

My idea

I am going to break into people's homes
and threaten them
and tie them up
Then I will do portraits of them
tied up
using oil paint
on canvas

I will make a number of these works
and I will show them
at a small commercial gallery space
in Piccadilly
The exhibition will be called *Portraits*

Bad

I eat insects
I do not mean to
They fly into my open mouth
I try to spit them out
But they seem to break apart
as soon as they enter my mouth
and I swallow parts of them by accident
It is quite unpleasant
They taste bad
and are of little nutritional value

Glue

Glue is now illegal
You can't buy it in the shops any more
If they find you gluing things
then you get into trouble
They don't want you to fix things
When things break
they want you to throw them away

You can make your own glue
in secret
and use it
But it's a risk

Politician

Stop all the injustice
Stop all the terrible things
that are happening
Replace all the bad things
with good things
So that everyone is happy
I can make this happen
Vote for me
as President of the World

Charging rhinoceros

Ignore the wild rhinoceros
that is charging towards you
If you ignore him
he will forget that you are there
and will charge at someone else
Take my advice
I have lived in the jungle for years
I know what I'm talking about
This is your only chance of survival

Information

I am on an aeroplane
flying high above you
The plane is full of bombs
and the hatch of the plane is open
and I'm standing right next to the bombs
And over the tannoy
the captain of the plane is saying:
'Go on, David, drop some bombs.'
And over the tannoy
the co-pilot of the plane is saying:
'Go on, David, drop some bombs.'
And the chief stewardess is saying:
'Go on, David, drop some bombs.'
And the other stewardesses are saying:
'Go on, David, drop some bombs.'
And some of the other passengers are saying:
'Go on, David, drop some bombs.'

So I'm probably going to drop some bombs on you
and I thought I'd better let you know

You don't know this but ...

There is a cave
in the centre of a thick forest
in the remotest part
of a remote island
off the coast of an uninhabited land
many miles away from anywhere
and very hard to get to

And in that cave
there is a huge immovable boulder
And buried deep in the ground
beneath that boulder
is a lead box
that is locked
and there is no key
And in that box
is an envelope
And in that envelope
there is a piece of paper
And on that piece of paper
is a small drawing
of what appears to be a smiley face

Read this

Read what I am writing
Pay close attention to the words
and to the meaning of the words
and how carefully they have been written
on my computer
while I was waiting
in the departure lounge
of an airport
for hours
and I had nothing else to do
and no pen to draw with
which is what I would rather have done
(drawing)

Ridicule

Water in the sea
comes up to my knee
because I am a giant

Clouds in the sky
I wonder why
they annoy me so

I will suck in all the clouds
Because I am a giant
(I told you that already)
and I have enormous lungs
and I will exhale the clouds
down your chimney
and it will rain inside your house
while you are in bed

It will be my revenge
because you have ridiculed me
for being a giant
I cannot help being a giant

The world

Give me a world
that is horrible and boring
and I will make it nice and interesting
I will paint it bright colours
for I am an artist
and that is what I do
Now shut up
and let me get on with my work
you idiot

Bruises

Bruises occur
when you bang a part of your body
against something hard
like a wall
or a door
or an anvil

Bruises can be removed
with a pencil eraser

Not many people know this
But it really works

Power cut

Watching a film
Enjoying it, etc.
Fifteen minutes left, roughly
Power cut
Lasts for hours
Candles, etc.
Hugely frustrating

Keep thinking about the film
Eventually
A few days later
Go to rental store
to rent the DVD
They have never heard of it
Look on the internet

No trace of the film
On the internet?
What the hell?
It must have been a dream

Dog's name

You buy a dog
You give it a name
The same name as one of your friends
The friend is offended
To hell with her!
She is no longer your friend

Mess

Mess
Where?
In the temple.
Should we clean it up?
No.
Why?
It is a holy mess.
So?
Only a priest can clear it up.
Is there nothing we can do?
We can pray.

Course of action

I chose a course of action
and I adhered to it with great rigidity
After some time had passed
I realised that my course of action
was at best very misguided
and at worst pathologically stupid
So I decided to halt my course of action
and I chose a new course of action
But after a while I realised
that my new course of action
was even more stupid than the first one
So I stopped that course of action too
And I got a job in a supermarket
with a view to saving up enough money
to go to teacher-training college

Laughter on the beach

I walked along the beach
and I found a beached whale rotting there
It was six metres long
It had a lady's sun hat perched on its head
It looked funny
and I laughed
I walked further along the beach
and I came upon a dead dolphin
It was wearing what appeared to be a floral-patterned dress
It looked funny
and I laughed
Never have I laughed so much
while walking on the beach
as I did that day

Hiding place

The monument to Lord Kitchener
on a clifftop
in the Orkney Islands
is like the large single turret of a castle
It is ten metres high
There is no door
or window
But you could probably get into it from above
if you had a big ladder
or if you were winched down from a helicopter
It would be a very good hiding place
A very good hiding place indeed

Shopping

Sifting through piles of junk
Trying to find something that you want
But you can't find anything that you want
Nothing at all
It's all junk

Say what you mean

It's better to say what you mean
and be despised for it
rather than to say what you don't mean as a joke
and be despised for it

Others

Do unto others
What you would have them do
unto you
Unless you are some kind of weird pervert
Who likes getting stabbed, etc.

Drinking

I drank wine
I got drunk
I wrote a play
It was awful
But it was popular

Life

Is there life on Mars?
No.
Is there life on any other planet except Earth?
No.
Are we the only life there is?
Yes.
Good. I am very glad.

Donkeys

What use are donkeys?

Donkeys are beasts of burden.
They pull things and carry things
so we don't have to.

I hate donkeys.

That is your choice.

The past

The past is gone
If you liked the past
then hard luck
It’s gone
and you had better get used to it

Warbling

Will you please stop warbling?
Warbling is undignified
and you are annoying me and
the other birds.

Blank page

I was reading a book
and I got to a blank page
I was angry
I took the book back to the shop
and demanded my money back
They said that it was not a mistake
That the blank page was supposed to be there
I said it was ridiculous
They gave me my money back

Info

There is too much info
There should be less
It would be better

Geese

Geese have long necks
and make an irritating sound
They are migratory birds
They live on water
Presumably they catch fish
That is all we know about them

Language

I invented my own language
I didn't like the other languages
So I invented my own
It has become hugely popular
Everybody uses it
and now I am rich

Truly rubbish

They told me my technique was truly rubbish
But they failed to acknowledge
that I do not profess to be anything other
than truly rubbish
and that I am almost entirely self-taught

Weather forecast

I am a cloud
I am full of rain
I'm telling you this
out of courtesy

Your journey

If there is anything I can do
to make your journey more comfortable
please tell me
But don't tell me yet
Because I am also on a journey
trying to be comfortable, etc.

Search engine

Ask me a question
any question
But make sure it's easy
I have only just begun
to answer questions
and I am not very good at it

Stupid

I'm not stupid
I'm pretending to be stupid
in order to gain an advantage
If you know what I mean

Good Lord!

What on earth are you doing?
You are taking a bath?
Why?
Because you are dirty?
I see.
Please leave the water in the tub
when you have finished.
I want to keep it.

Listen

Some things don't work
You will find this out
You think that everything works
But you are wrong
Some things don't work

Deception

I am not trying to deceive you
I would not do that
I am just playing a trick

I am learning to be a magician
I recently lost my job
and need to find a new source of income

Inspiration

I take inspiration from everywhere:
overheard conversations
found letters
graffiti
classical music
the behaviour of animals
But I am frequently discouraged
and rarely produce anything

The end

My battery is running out
and I don't have the means to recharge it
This is not an excuse
It is a valid reason
for me to stop

Literature

I wrote a lot
It was all rubbish
I threw it away
before anyone could read it

Congratulations

Very good
Excellent
Bravo!
Now go away

Touching dirt

Touch the dirt
Feel it
Do you like it?
You do like it!
Are you surprised that you like it?
You are surprised that you like it!
You thought that you wouldn't like it!
I knew you would like the dirt
I know you better than you know yourself
I am like an adult
and you are like my baby
touching the dirt
under my supervision

Life

Plant life
trying to grow
Animals
trying to breed
All this is made difficult
by you
and your public art project

Inspection

I did an inspection
I inspected you
while you were asleep
You appear to be in good order
I was impressed
I will inspect you again
in about a year
while you are asleep

Let me splain

I felt the laddar
n I bonged my nut
nfact I nutted the floor
nnow I been made a fool
see
nnow I cat think proppery

Nice paper

I always write on nice paper
If ever I don't
There is a reason

Reality

Reality falls on top of you
and breaks your collarbone
and one of your toes
You should have got out of the way
of reality
You were warned
several times
by me
and others

Sat nav

I have no idea of our current location
We could be anywhere
I know this is disappointing news
and I am sorry

The melons

Walking among the ripe melons
in the melon patch
I am struck by how beautiful they are
I reach down to touch one
It is cold
and a bit slimy

I am repulsed
and I run from the melon patch
screaming at the top of my lungs
My friend is disappointed with me
He was enjoying the peace of the melon patch
So was I
But then I touched one of those awful things

Pond

What is at the end of the rainbow?
At the end of the rainbow there is a pond.
A pond?
Yes.
I thought there would be a pot of gold.
No. There is a pond.

Things cometh

Wonderful things
cometh
We should wait for them
quietly
in our dens
and we should not bark
or howl
Or we may scare off
the wonderful things
and other dogs will get them

Overwhelmed

Overwhelming nonsense
everywhere
We cannot hide from it
The only thing to do
is to become part of it

Data

Data-entry people
entering data
They are happy
They like doing it
while we play sports

Trust

When you get to the front of the queue
please buy me a hotdog
I will pay you for it
have no fear
for I am a reliable
and trustworthy
man

Instructions

Hold the stick firmly in both hands
Do not let it slip from your grasp
If it slips from your grasp
then it is lost
and you will not get another one
The mixture will be stiff at first
but will soon yield to the stick
Stir the mixture
until it froths violently
Open the cage of rodents
and pour them into the mixture
continue to stir
Chant the incantation
until the ghostly faces start to appear
Remove the mixture from the heat
and allow it to cool
before pouring into bowls
and serving with crusty bread

Marbles

Get your marbles out
I want to play marbles
Get them on the floor
Kneel down
You go first
Now I go
I win
You owe me £100

Bee

Bumble bee
Bumble bee
Buzz on over
here to me
Bumble bee
Bumble bee
See if you can land on my penis

Where are we going?
Does the pilot know?
I don't think he does
He just likes flying
He will keep going
until we run out of fuel
and crash
I would like to go and speak to him
but nobody is allowed in the cockpit
except the pilot

The mirror

The mirror was hung on the wall in a stupid way
I looked in it and saw that I had long hair
I had no recollection of having grown it long
I looked in the wardrobe
It was full of women's clothes
I tried on a dress
It did not fit
But still I wore it
I went outside
It was a cold day
and my nipples became hard
and I was self-conscious of them
On my feet were rubber boots
There was some kind of parade going on
I walked past a man who was completely naked
apart from a cowboy hat
and he said to me
'nice tits'
and I said 'thank you'
I could not think of anything amusing to say to him
There were other naked men around
some of them were very attractive
but, in truth, I found the whole thing quite vulgar
I went back to the house
and went back to bed
and went to sleep
and when I woke up
everything was back to normal

The enormous thing

To whom does this enormous thing belong?
I would like to know
It needs to be removed
as it is blocking my rear entrance
I rarely moan about such things
but on this occasion I am compelled
to moan
I am expecting a delivery
and the only way it can go in
is through my rear entrance
And if this thing is not removed
before the delivery arrives
then I shall not be a happy man

The dirt

The dirt
Oh
The dirt
I am king of it
I have power
over it
It must yield
to me
I collect it
and remove it
from your house

It is my job

Skinny man
You will have your day
I will see to that
I'll feed you on pies and sausage rolls
I will make you fat

Skinny man
Oh skinny friend
A good friend you have made
for I have access to pastry stuffs
so be thou not afraid

Me/you

I am me
you are you
it is okay

You must stay as you
you cannot be me
that would not be okay

I do not want to be you
I will not allow it
It will not happen

Later …
It now appears that I am you
and you are me
It is not okay
but I must accept it

Know this

Know this.
It cometh.
You cannot
stop it.
You must accept it.

Go to hell

Go to hell
I've been to hell
You will like hell
I can recommend hell
Take my advice
and go to hell

Forest-dwellers

We who live in the forest
we do not ask much from you
You who live in the city
we only ask
that you stop laughing at us
and that you stop taking photographs of us
whilst we are performing our rituals

Friends

You can never have enough friends
I feel that I have too few friends
I roam the streets at night
looking for friends
I always find at least one friend every night
I invite them back to my house
and we sometimes play cards
or sometimes I kill them
Killing friends is not good
I know this
but
I don't care

Film review

I watched the film
I did not like it
I did not like the actors
They reminded me of real people
and I did not like the things they said
The special effects were also too realistic
It was like reality
especially because it was in 3D
This was not what I wanted
I was disappointed
and I suggest you do not go to see the film
Apparently it will win Oscars

Dancing

They are rocking in the jungle
All the animals are dancing
and the indigenous people are dancing
and the animals are dancing at the zoo
because the zoo is near the jungle
and the zoo animals can hear the music
And in the prison there is also music
they are dancing there
some together, some alone
And there is music at the school
The children are dancing
and it is getting out of hand
and the teacher has to bash them with a stick
And there is music in the office
and all the men and women in suits are dancing
and they are drunk
And where the soldiers live
they are dancing
Someone is beating a drum
and they are firing their guns in time
and also firing a big cannon
and they are having a terrific time
and they are laughing
And they are rocking and rolling in the hospital
and the doctors and nurses are dancing
but mostly the patients aren't dancing
because they are ill or dying

And they are dancing on the highway
and it is dangerous
And up in the sky the passengers in planes
are dancing
and the pilots are dancing
to the sound of rock music
and it is dangerous
and I really think it should stop
it should stop right now
On ships in the sea they are dancing
and on oil rigs they are dancing
even though they are covered in oil
And in parliament they are dancing
all the politicians
when they should be running the country
and the police station
the police are dancing
when they should be catching criminals
and in gardens and in palaces and other countries
and in warehouses
they are all dancing
letting their hair down
and in orphanages and in abattoirs and in churches
and in shops
they are all bloody well dancing
And I can't join in and it is making me crazy
because I twisted my ankle and it is very sore

Throw away your drugs

Throw away your tabs of acid
throw away your lines of coke
throw away your heroin needles
throw away all forms of dope

You don't need them any more
There's other things to occupy you
good things on the television
good things on the internet

There are programmes about cooking
there are home renovation shows
there are programmes about prisons and gypsies
there are programmes about real life

Throw away your magic mushrooms
throw away your horse tranquillizers
throw away your pipes and bongs
throw away your ecstasy

You don't need them any more
There's other things to occupy you
good things on the television
good things on the internet

There are sexual problems programmes
shows about what fat people eat
there are programmes about Hitler
there are programmes about real life

Throw away your crack pipe medicine
throw away your hallucinogenic toads
throw away your speedball cocktail
throw away your opium

You don't need them any more
There's other things to occupy you
good things on the television
good things on the internet

good things on the television
good things on the internet

Choose your weapon

Choose your weapon:
axe
or spoon?
I have already chosen the axe.
You must take the spoon.
It will be a fair fight
because the axe is blunt
and the spoon is sharp.
Are you ready?

Battle

Knight in shining armour
Where are you going
on your horse
with its long mane?
Are you going to battle?
I am assuming so
on account of your armour's shine.
Don't let me detain you.
On you go.
I shall be interested to know
how you get on.

My brain is working just fine
thank you very much for asking
I have no difficulty in processing
or retaining information
no difficulty at all
and I don't have any difficulty
in expressing myself
my brain is working just fine
thank you

My brain is working just fine
thank you very much for asking
I have no difficulty in processing
or retaining information
no difficulty at all
and I don't have any difficulty
in expressing myself
my brain is working just fine
thank you

My brain is working just fine
thank you very much for asking
I have no difficulty in processing
or retaining information
no difficulty at all
and I don't have any difficulty
in expressing myself
my brain is working just fine
thank you

Mother, you can't be in the band

It all started a few weeks ago
It was early one morning
and the telephone started to ring
So I went downstairs
and I answered it
and it was my mother calling from Munich
I had told her the week before that I was in a band
She said she had been thinking
that she would like to be in the band
even though she can't play anything
She decided that she would like to play the drums
The drums? She wants to play the drums?
But I said that we already have a drummer
So she said that we should get rid of him
So I said we can't do that
He's a really good drummer
and you have never played the drums
You have never even tried to play the drums
Our drummer has been playing for more than thirty years
We can't just get rid of him
Because he's a really good drummer

Mother, you can't be in the band
Mother, you can't be in the band
We already have a drummer
He is an excellent drummer
so, Mother, you can't be in the band
Mother, you can't be in the band

So then she said
why don't we have two drummers in the band?
Like the Glitter Band, they were a really good band
But I said no, we are not that kind of band
Nobody wants to be compared to the Glitter Band now
and she said why not?
So I told her why not
So she said what about Adam and the Ants?
They had two drummers and they are still cool
So I said yes, but that's not really the point
Nobody wants to be in a band with their mum, right?
That's definitely not cool
So she said something quite unkind to me
about me being bald
so I said

Mother, you can't be in the band
Mother, you can't be in the band
We already have a drummer
We don't need another drummer
We don't want two drummers
so, Mother, you can't be in the band
Mother, you can't be in the band

So then she said she would like to play the guitar
She said any idiot can play the guitar
She sees people wandering around the streets with guitar cases
all the time and they look like they are probably morons
I said they are not morons they are musicians
So she said maybe she could play the bass
bass players are definitely morons
It would be easy for her to learn
The bass only has four strings
How hard can it be?
But I said no
It is really difficult to learn those instruments
and besides we already have enough people playing
those instruments
So she said maybe she could play the keyboards because that
looks really easy
and I said no
It's not easy, it's really hard
So she said maybe she could move the equipment
and I said we don't need anyone to move the equipment
Especially not an elderly person
So then she said she could drive the van
So I said no, no, no.

Mother, you can't be in the band
Mother, this is getting out of hand
Mother, we don't need you in the band
Mother, we don't want you in the band
so, Mother, you can't be in the band
Mother, you can't be in the band

Potato peeling
Peculiar feeling
Lying on the ceiling
English mustard
in your custard
Mayonnaise sunscreen
Dye your hair green
What does it mean?
Collecting earthworms for your tea
Wounds are sewn up
Plate of donuts
haven't yet shown up
I'd like to buy
a snooker cue

Kitchen utensil
Cat's gone mental
Bendy pencil
Delivering pamphlets
Take your tablets
Lost in thick fog
Feed your hotdog
to a hedgehog
Keep your thoughts in a polythene bag
Morons dancing
quite entrancing
life enhancing
What if I fall
in a pond?

1 2 3 4
what are we here for?
5 6 7 8
shut your gob

Can't stop winking
Brains are shrinking
Lights are blinking
Mowing my lawn
Eating frogspawn
Chewing dog bones
Idiots I've known
wearing earphones
Give me back my wellington boot
Don't be boring
Stick your oar in
Eat your portion
I seem to have lost my floppy hat

Quite distracting
Legs need waxing
Tooth extracting
Play your bagpipes
under floodlights
Mental breakdown
Running round town
dressed as a clown
Living in a dungeon underground
Maybe baby
You've got rabies
Taste my gravy
Who's that standing in our porch?

1 2 3 4
what are we here for?
5 6 7 8
shut your gob

Obstacles

Sometimes obstacles they are tiny
Sometimes obstacles are huge
Sometimes people are nice to you
and then sometimes they are rude

Sometimes you get attacked by children
Sometimes you get attacked by dwarves
Sometimes they bite you on your ankles
Sometimes they scratch you with their claws

    Sometimes you slip on a banana
    Sometimes you slip upon the ice
    Sometimes you fall without reason
    Sometimes you collapse because you're drunk

    Sometimes you fall from a ladder
    Sometimes you fall down a hole
    Sometimes you have to go for treatment
    Sometimes you get arrested by the police

Sometimes the rain goes down the drainpipe
Sometimes it flows into the drain
Sometimes filth comes up through the floorboards
They say it has to do with climate change

Sometimes the sky turns to orange
Sometimes the sky turns to red
Sometimes the sky turns to purple
Eventually we will all be dead

Sometimes they take you to the nuthouse
Sometimes they shave off all your hair
Often they take away your clothing
Most people don't know why they're there

Rubbish is strewn around the pavement
Wild dogs are roaming around the streets
This is the end of civilisation
Cannibals are moving in next door

Sometimes obstacles they are tiny
Sometimes obstacles are huge
Sometimes people are nice to you
and then sometimes they are rude

I am very much in love with you

If you were glue
I would sniff you
If you were vodka
I would spill you
If you were some kind of gas
I'd inhale you

    I am very much in love with you
    I am deeply obsessed with you

If you were drugs
I would take you
If you were medicine
I would also take you
If you were ointment
I would apply you
carefully
to my wounds

    I am very much in love with you
    I am deeply obsessed with you
    I think about you all the time

If you were food
I would eat you
If you were a cigar
I would smoke you
after dinner
If you were a prisoner
I would free you from your cage

I'd free you from your rat-infested cage
so that we could be together
and then you would be mine
and we would both be really happy

If you were a flower
I would help you grow
If you were a small animal
I would protect you from predators
If you were a warehouse
I would guard you

I am very much in love with you
I am deeply obsessed with you
I think about you all the time

If you were a song
I would try to sing you
If you were a flute
I would learn to play you
If you were a book
I would burn you

I am very much in love with you
I am deeply obsessed with you
I think about you all the time
and you make me really happy

If you were a pen
I would write with you
If you were a hat
I would wear you
If you were gossip
I would share you on the internet

I am very much in love with you
I would like to keep you in my cellar
I would never ever ever ever
ever let you out

If you were a hairstyle
I would imitate you
If you were a clone
I would replicate you
If you were an illness
I would die from you

I am very much in love with you
I am deeply obsessed with you
I think about you all the time
and you make me really happy

Flea on the dog

I am a flea on a very big dog
I bite the dog and drink his blood
but the dog he does not notice
and it makes me very angry

I am a bubble in your drink
Being a bubble makes me laugh
Being a bubble I follow my path
and I rise to the surface and I pop

I am a worm beneath the earth
All the soil will pass through me
in the winter and the summer
in one end and out the other

I have forgotten where I live
I have forgotten my wife's name
I have forgotten my own name
But I remember everything else

I'm just like everyone else
I'm just like everyone else
I'm just like everyone else

You are not like everyone else
You are not like everyone else

I have high-speed internet
and many expensive pairs of shoes
a jacuzzi and a guinea pig
a sports car and an antique pistol

I can play the xylophone
I once ate a centipede
It tasted like metal and
it left a stain upon my hand

Mummy beat me with a stick
Mummy hit me hard with it
I punched Mummy in the tit
Mummy stabbed me with a fork

Someone slashed my daddy's tyre
Daddy told me I'm a liar
Daddy set my toys on fire
Daddy tied me up with wire

I will deal with all my problems
I will deal with unwanted thoughts
I will imagine that they are crockery
I will smash them with a hammer

I'm just like everyone else
I'm just like everyone else
I'm just like everyone else

You are not like everyone else
You are not like everyone else

Boots shoes

Ballet shoe
Gladiator sandal
Chelsea boot
Brogues
Wellington boot
Pumps
Clogs
Brothel creeper
Running shoe

What have you been walking on?
Gravel?
Nice

Tennis shoe
Espadrilles
Moccasins
Gym shoe
Pixie boots
Flip flops
Gym shoe
Disposable slipper

What have you been wading through?
Rice pudding?
Excellent

Hobnail boot
Winkle-picker
Tap shoes
Slip-ons
Platform soles
Loafers
Stack heels
Rugby boot
Ice skates

What have you been walking on?
Laminated flooring?
Classy!

Kinky boots
Deck shoes
Dr. Martens –
18-holers
Ugg boots
Slingbacks
High tops
Dirty socks

What have you been walking on?
Broken crockery?
That's risky!

Bowling shoes
Plastic sandals
Roller blades
Plimsolls
Moon boots
Flippers
Glass slippers
Bare feet
Clown shoes

What have you been wading through?
Animal faeces?
Bravo!

Skanky footgear
Running spikes
Snow boots
Wing tips
Clodhoppers
Shitkickers
Court shoes
Birkenstocks

What have you been walking on?
Sticky carpet!
Alright!

Shoes
Boots
Boots and shoes
Put your socks on
Put your shoes on
Put your boots on
Take your boots off
Take your socks off

What size are you?

No vacancies

Don't sleep in the comfy chair
there's no space for you there
so don't you dare

Don't sleep on the sofa bed
there's no place for you there
there's a child sleeping there

Don't sleep in the dog's bed
there's a dog sleeping there
there's no room for you there

Don't sleep in the corridor
there's a man sleeping there
and he'll pull your hair

Don't sleep in the entrance hall
there's a drunk sleeping there
and it's a fire risk

Don't sleep in the garden shed
Grandad's in there
and he'll kick you in the head

Don't sleep in the middle of the road
it's a busy road
and you'll get squashed

The party is over
and all the booze is gone
and you've been here for hours

Don't sleep on the grassy knoll
there's an assassin sleeping there
and you should keep away from him

Don't sleep in the paddling pool
there are frogs breeding there
and you'll get covered in slime

Don't sleep in the treehouse
it's in a tree
and it's not a real house

Go away please go away
It's time for you to go home
Please bugger off

Dear brain

Dear Brain
I know that you are lord of everything that I do
and that I must obey you
and that you and I are one
and there is nothing that can be done about it
but oh dear brain please hear my request
that you stop making me say things that I don't mean
and that you stop making me do things that I don't want to do
because if it were up to me I wouldn't say and do all
those things
all those terrible things that have got me into such
terrible trouble
I would behave more nicely
and I would not be violent or abusive to strangers
and I would wear clothes and I would not steal things
or burn things or kill things
but oh dear brain I know that you know what is best for me
even though I cannot see the wisdom in the things you make
me do
I know that it is your will that always prevails
and it is not for me to know your purpose
but oh dear lord brain please hear me when I ask
if it is your will
please oh brain stop making me behave like such a degenerate
for I am thy kingdom aren't I? I am
Thank you
Amen

The catastrophe

Please do not say
that you are enjoying the catastrophe
It is not helpful
Please keep quiet about it
or lie about your true feelings
Thank you

Baggage reclaim

When you have landed
and have alighted the aircraft
You must
reclaim your baggage
from the carousel
You cannot leave it behind
This is not allowed
You must take it
and carry it with you
always

The food

When it arrived
we found that
the food bore no resemblance
to the food pictured on the menu
and it tasted horrible
But the service was swift
and the cutlery was clean

Trust yourself

You are trustworthy
I think it is fairly unlikely
that you would lie to yourself
I think you can trust yourself
for the most part
I could be wrong
but I don't think I am

Just cause

It is a just cause
that I am fighting for
I have researched it
quite a bit
and now I know
who my enemies are
and why they must be destroyed

Snowman

I built a snowman
I did not know how to do it at first
But there was a man who helped me
It was very kind of him
I gave him some money

The truth

I am acquainted with the truth
but we are not friends
We used to be friends
but then
all of a sudden
the truth was very unkind to me
and now we are estranged
I regret this
but it appears we shall never be reconciled

The sponge

The sponge soaks up all the goop
That is the purpose of the sponge
Without the sponge
the goop would be a problem
We could be submerged
and we don't want that
so let's be thankful for the sponge
and stop disrespecting it

Paradise

What the hell am I doing
going to that place
on the plane?
Am I mad?
I have no reason to go
but still I am going
I know what it will be like
I know it will be disappointing
but still I am going

Clouds

Sometimes viewed when outside
Sometimes viewed through the window
Sometimes taking pleasing forms
that give me great joy
Sometimes taking offensive forms
that I am troubled by
Oh how I wish I knew
what they were going to do
I would be much less anxious

Pleased to meet you

Very pleased.
Can I ask
where did you get that hat
with the peacock feather in it?
Rarely do you see young men
with such hats
these days.
From a shop?
It was going cheap?
I see.
You are a fortunate young man.
Close the door.
Close the window.
Lift the rug.
Get under the rug
so you are completely covered
and all we can see is the vague shape of you.
Now sing a song
preferably a folk song.
There: that's good.
I am really impressed by your talent
and your form.

Today

Today I feel so fragile
like the wing of a moth
that will be irreparably damaged
if you touch it
But yesterday
I felt indestructible
like a giant war-robot
So I went to the pub
and got drunk

Wine

The arrangement we had
I thought
was that you would provide me
with several bottles of wine
Instead
you have provided me
with a bucket of water
You are fortunate
that I am the Messiah
and am able to deal with the situation

Please

Do not cheer
when the coffin goes past
Do not laugh
when they read the prayer
Do not dance a jig
at the graveside
Do not get drunk
and vomit
in the grave

I have a plan

Tons of plastic crap
in the ocean
Tons of poison
in the river
Tons of the wrong kind of gas
in the atmosphere
Lots of dog shit
in the park
I have a plan
to sort it all out
and I'm starting with the dog shit

Repair

Fabergé Egg
sat on a wall
Fabergé Egg
had a great fall
All the conservators
from the museum
have been working on it
and it will be repaired
in time for the Easter holiday

Long and joyful

Glum look
upon your face
changes to a broad smile
when I light a fart
I know how to make you happy
and we will have a long and joyful marriage
I am sure

Puffy features

They were a bit puffy
then
they became quite puffy
recently
They were not puffy prior to that
I want you to know that
and
that
the puffiness will diminish
at some point
before long
but I don't know exactly when

Outcomes

It does things to you
when you go on the fairground rides
Sometimes you go on and you're tall
and when you come off you're small
and sometimes vice versa
Sometimes you go on and you're thin
and you come off and you're fat
and so on
Sometimes you come off and you've laid an egg
in your pants (a chicken's egg)
and sometimes your hair changes colour
and sometimes you turn into a bat (it happened once)
and sometimes you go on with dirty clothes
and when you come off they're clean
spotless in fact
This is the best outcome

Order

What will you order from the menu?
Nothing.
Nothing?
Nothing.
How do you want it cooked?
I'd like it raw.

It's okay to eat doughnuts

It's okay to smoke cigars
It's okay to wear a dress (regardless of your gender)
It's okay to talk to yourself
All these things are totally fine and acceptable
To find a list of the things that aren't acceptable
please refer to our website

Dream diary

I kept a diary of my dreams
for many years
My house was robbed
and the diary was stolen
and later was put on the internet
for all too see
I was upset at the time
but now
I actually feel quite proud

The stupid song

Takes a stupid man
to sing a stupid song
Takes a stupid man
to sing a stupid song
Takes a stupid man
to sing a stupid song
Let us all be hopeful
that he won't sing it for long

Crumbs of comfort

I love the crumbs of comfort
I gather them up
I seek them out
from under the furniture
the sofa
the bed
the Welsh dresser
the barrel organ
They are delicious
The supply seems endless
I have never cleaned the house
though
I am shortly to be married
and I am unsure how my wife will react
when she sees me licking crumbs off the floor
I would value your opinion on this matter

Decision

I will not be told what to do any more
I used to like to be told
what to do
but now I have figured out what I like doing
So unless you're going to tell me to do that
then I will not be told what to do

Sounds

Whilst in a castle
I dropped a spanner
on the marble floor
and I liked the sound
so much
that I have decided to incorporate it
into one of my performances
The next show
is at Westminster Abbey
on Thursday night
Please come along
The opening act
is a bell-ringer

Overhead

I fly high
over rough terrain
in my solar-powered plane
I look down
I see you
camping
I shout
but you don't hear
you are busy
digging a hole
to shit in

Studio

What can you see
when you look through the keyhole?
Can you see the artist sharpening his pencil?
Can you see him preparing to draw
the big hairy nude model?
Can you see the drawing?
Is it a good drawing?
Would you like to buy it?
It will cost you a thousand pounds.
And that's with discount.
How would you like to pay?

Final word

I have nothing left to say
except
please could you remove your bicycle
from the side passage
and please could you leave the bins out
on Tuesday
and please could you water the plants
and mow the lawn
and cut the hedge
and do the laundry
and read my thesis
and tell me what you think of it
(please be specific)

Feelings

I feel like a dog
fetching a ball
I also feel like a hamster
in a wheel
and I also feel like a bird in a cage
and a kite in the wind
and I also feel like an elephant
trampling a village
and I feel like a snake in the grass
and an otter in the stream
and a rat in the bin
and I am also tired
and quite hungry

Let me paint you a picture

What kind of picture?
A landscape.
Will I be in it?
Do you want to be in it?
Yes.
Then you shall be in it.
(later)
Here's your picture.
Where am I?
You are not in it.
Why not?
Because you're an asshole.

The cold light of day

Things look different
in the cold light of day
I now see that things are
much less awful
than I thought they were

Giant ball rolling down the hill

Giant ball rolling down the hill
destroying the stuff in its path
trees
houses
cars
I was at the top of the hill
and I pushed the ball
and set it rolling
I now realise
what a reckless act it was
and I regret it
I was trying to impress a young lady
whom I am in love with

The hissing sound

It is hard to identify
where it is coming from
It seems to come from everywhere
and I am at a loss as
to know what to do about it
The dreadful smell
surrounds us completely
I don't know what it is
or where it is coming from
All I know
is that it is dreadful
and that it surrounds us completely
But the vibrations
I rather like the vibrations
I find them comforting

Clown food

What do clowns eat?
Clown food.
What does it taste like?
It tastes funny.
Are you being serious?
No. I am joking.
So you know nothing of clowns and their ways?
I know they are funny.
That is not always true.
Yes. You are right. I am sorry.

The red cord

The red cord
hanging down
do not pull it
unless you are in need of medical assistance
The panic button
beneath the desk
do not push it
unless you are in danger
The flare
in the emergency bag
do not light it
unless you are lost
and need to be rescued
The bottle of wine
in the cupboard
do not drink it
or I will crush you like an insect
It is mine
and I need it
you fucker

Here I am

Right here
In front of you
Can you see me?
Why can't you see me?
Are you blind?
Why can't you see me?
Are you stupid?
Why can't you see me?
Here I am
Right here
In front of you

Your old songs

You wrote some songs
long ago
It was the only thing you did
that people actually liked
Everything you have done since
has been rubbish
Many times you have been told
to stop doing the rubbish things
and just sing your old songs
But you never listened
and you carried on
creating rubbish
But now at last
you are singing your old songs again
Thank goodness

The slope

Marbles
Ping pong balls
Golf balls
Pebbles
Potatoes
Vegan meat balls
Quail eggs
All rolling
down a slope
It would seem inevitable
that the golf balls
will get to the bottom first
But things don't always turn out
as you would expect them to

Announcement

I am glad to have been of service
to you
However I must now inform you
That I will not be of service any more
I have decided to serve myself
from now on
so you must clean up your own shit
from now on
Thank you

Crust

The crust is good
Tastes good
Smells good
Looks good
If you're going to cut it off
and discard it
then give it to me
I'll have it

Surfboards

I have many surfboards
but I have never surfed
and I have many guitars
though I do not know how to play them
and I have a number of cars
though I cannot drive
and I have a collection of combs
though I am completely bald
and I have lots of clothes
though I mostly walk around naked
and to be honest
almost all the things I have
I do not need
So I am going to sell everything on eBay
and start my own religion

I never think about complicated things

I only think about simple things
like breathing
and eating
so please remember this
before you interact with me
thanks

Bastards!

Those terrible bastards!
I wish I wasn't in love with them
They are such terrible bastards
I wish I did not worship them
like gods
Those terrible bastards
I wish I did not think about them
all the time
and constantly draw pictures of them
and exhibit them in art galleries
and I wish I did not make
such a fine living
from drawing pictures of those
terrible bastards

The big thing

Stop thinking about
the big thing
Thinking about it
constantly
will do you no good
Think about
other things
and in doing so
it may change your attitude towards
the big thing

Hidden inside

Reveal your inner self
They said
Not likely I said
My inner self must remain hidden I said
But we want to see it
They said
We are intrigued by your output and must know
where it comes from –
the source of the output
They said
Well I'm not revealing my inner self I said
So you'll just have to be satisfied with my output
as it is
I said

The words

I do not know what to do
with the words I have written
DELETE THEM!
the voices shout
I WILL NOT DELETE THEM!
I shout
WHO THE HELL ARE YOU TALKING TO?
my husband asks
JUST THINKING ALOUD
I reply
I will keep writing
until I figure out what to do
A blog perhaps

In the beginning

there was light
It was I who turned the light on
Everyone was scrabbling about in the dark
and when I turned the light on
they were all embarrassed
because they became aware they had been scrabbling about
and it was undignified
and I made them realise this
And I am quite proud of this
even though they show me no gratitude